What Your Boss Never Wants You to Know

How to Find Your Strengths, Work Happier, Grow Your Expertise, and Rediscover Your Life

Lam Thanh Hue

Table of contents

Introduction 1

PART I.. 5

WHAT WILL MAKE US HAPPY? 5

    Chapter 1 We Are Conditioned to Want "Normal" 6

    Chapter 2 But Is "Normal" Really What We Want? 14

    Chapter 3 Discovering What We Do Want....................................... 26

    Chapter 4 How Big Do We Dare to Dream? 35

    Chapter 5 Changing Our Mindset 42

    Chapter 6 Taking the Leap 54

PART II *WHAT YOUR BOSS NEVER*

WANTS YOU TO KNOW 64

    Chapter 7 We Work to Serve Others.. 65

    Chapter 8 No One Is Happy Until They Learn to Serve

    Themselves 71

    Chapter 9 Understand the Roles that Fear and Desire Play in Life

    75

    Chapter 10 What Truly Motivates Us?.. 80

    Chapter 11 How to Work for Oneself in Someone Else's

    Company 86

PART III *WHEN WORKING WITH PASSION MEANS*

BEING OUR OWN BOSSES... 92

Chapter 12 Am I an Entrepreneur? 93

Chapter 13 Finding Ways to Make Money

Doing What One Loves..100

Chapter 14 Kill Procrastination..106

Chapter 15 Setting a Work Schedule that Works for the

Individual..111

Chapter 16 Set SMART Goals 115

Chapter 17 Always Have a Plan 121

PART IV *WORK HACKS TO WORK LESS AND ENJOY LIFE*

MORE... 124

Chapter 18 Creating Passive Income.................................125

Chapter 19 Helpful Tools and Services 132

Chapter 20 Giving the Workspace a Makeover 137

Chapter 21 Surrounding Oneself with Positivity..............142

Chapter 22 Becoming Location-Independent...............146

Chapter 23 Always Seek to Improve..................................150

Conclusion 155

About the Author 157

Introduction

Before we get started, I would like to thank and congratulate you for downloading your copy of *What Your Boss Never Wants You to Know: How to Find Your Strengths, Work Happier, Grow Your Expertise, and Rediscover Your Life*. In this brief but information-packed guide, we will follow the story of a fictional character named Hula as she awakens to her true feelings about her life. We will discuss how Hula learns valuable lessons about personal fulfillment and finds deeper meaning through work and her career.

Too many of us find ourselves in the situation of feeling unfulfilled in life. Perhaps we are lucky enough to land the job of our dreams, to find someone we want to spend the rest of our lives with, and to enjoy the blessings of a loving family. For so many of us, something still compels us to want more. Is it a fact of the human condition that we will always be unsatisfied with what we have, or are we simply not taught how to find that satisfaction in our daily lives?

One thing that is certain is that most of us need to work to survive. Some latch onto whatever job they can find to make ends meet and get by. Others pour countless hours into gaining the education, skills, and experience that they need to find a position that will reward them with material gains and a sense of meaning. In both cases, these people too often end up feeling bored, dissatisfied, and ultimately trapped in a position that isn't bringing them happiness or enhancing their lives the way they would like.

So, what is missing? What are all these people doing wrong? How can so many be unhappy in a time when technology and the abundance of available information make nearly anything possible?

The short answer is that they are not asking themselves the right questions, and therefore they are not digging deep enough. Many people avoid asking the right questions because their fear of not knowing how to move forward with the answers prevents them from stirring things up.

While each individual's path is as unique as the person walking it, people tend to fall into two categories when it comes to work: they either choose to work within an organization, or they choose to create their own as an entrepreneur. In this book, Hula will explore both paths as she strives to discover what it is that she truly wants in life and how she needs to get it.

Part I

What Will Make Us Happy?

Chapter 1
We Are Conditioned to Want "Normal"

If we ask people what the definition of success is, chances are that many will recite a list of luxury goods: fancy cars, a giant house, housekeepers and gourmet chefs, private yachts and jets, and five-star vacations. Ask those same people what they want in life and they'll probably say something like: to find a well-paying job, to settle down with a life partner, to buy a house in a good part of town, to start a family, and to retire as young as possible. Press those people with a deeper question such as, "What is the meaning of life?" and the response will likely be something along the lines of "to find a purpose in the world" or "to do meaningful work."

Of course, there is no right or wrong answer to any of these questions. However, for many, the answer to one question is often the answer to all three. The sense of purpose or meaning often comes from the type of work one chooses to do, and if it does not come from there, one hopes to find it in domestic and personal life.

While there are many individuals who will express different answers to those same questions, in industrial society, at least, the answers tend to be very similar. Perhaps people assume that because "everyone" follows this formula to find happiness and fulfillment, it must bring them what they seek. Or perhaps people simply want to fit in with their peers and to do what is expected of them. They want to be seen as "normal."

From the time that we are young, our parents and relatives begin to groom us into a life of security and conventional wisdom. For many of them, they grew up seeing that a certain path led to the greatest success in life, and whether or not they followed that path, the formula stuck with them and they passed it on to their children.

Hula's parents were no different. Ever since she was a little girl, they pressed the importance of getting good grades, attending a prestigious college, and starting an honorable career. Her mother was a nurse and her father worked for an insurance company. Together they raised their children with the values of hard work and integrity.

When she was very young, Hula confided to her mother that she wanted to be an artist when she grew up. Her mother made a disapproving face and told her that artists don't make any money and that she should be a doctor or a lawyer instead. At this impressionable age, Hula learned that her passion and creativity were less important than the size of her salary. She resolved to focus her efforts only on the things that would bring her material success, and though she enjoyed different artistic hobbies in her limited free time, she never again considered art as a viable career path.

Though she turned her back on the artist's path, Hula couldn't help but be attracted to potential careers that would give her the opportunity to exercise her creative abilities and earn a decent salary to make her parents proud. In high school, she took an elective class in marketing and discovered that advertising might hold the key to her different desires. She could use her artistic abilities to design ads for a marketing firm while also earning a high-paying salary working for an established and reputable company that would offer her long-term security.

Hula graduated high school at the top of her class and went on to college, where she double majored in marketing and graphic design. She was so busy with her heavy workload that she often found herself rushing through her design projects, never spending as much time on any project as much as she would have liked. She consoled herself by telling herself she'd have plenty of time to focus on individual projects once she got hired by a firm and tried to be content with doing enough to get passing grades.

Her hard work paid off and before she knew it, Hula graduated college and landed an amazing internship at a reputable marketing firm in New York City. The thrill of realizing her dream pushed her through the long hours at the office and the even longer hours at the coffee shop she worked at to make ends meet. It was here that she met the handsome young professional who would eventually become her husband.

At the end of her internship, Hula's dreams were realized when she was offered a permanent position with the firm. Shortly after, her boyfriend proposed and the two were soon married. They lived happily in the city, sharing an apartment as they grew their careers. After a couple of years, when their careers were well-established and the timing felt right, the two agreed that it was time to start a family. They purchased a house in the suburbs and commuted every day to work in the city. After months of meticulous research, they had found the best school district in the state and settled down to raise their children with every opportunity available to them.

Hula and her husband each labored to climb the corporate ladder, and each experienced plenty of success. Eventually, Hula was promoted to manage a marketing team for a large client, and though she missed the hands-on role of designing ads, she enjoyed the added perks of higher pay and greater benefits. As her investment portfolio grew, she rested easier knowing that she and her children would be taken care of in the future.

On the outside, Hula's life appeared to be one of great success. She had graduated from a great college, landed her dream job, and was working her way up the corporate ladder in what was proving to be a fruitful and successful career. Hula enjoyed reading books and magazines on business, marketing, and self-improvement in her free time, and when she had the rare afternoon or evening to herself, she even managed to find the time to draw or paint. Her husband and children were a great source of pride to her, and she cherished the annual family vacations they took whenever time and their busy schedules allowed. The family lived a relatively normal and peaceful life, and they fit in well with their friends and neighbors.

Yes, on the surface, everything looked perfect. But, as Hula was soon to discover, appearances can be deceiving.

Chapter 2
But Is "Normal" Really What We Want?

Although anyone looking on from the outside might have said that Hula lived the "perfect" life, she was soon to discover that things were not as they seemed. Looking back later she saw that all the warning signs had been there for some time. With the demands of her busy career and family life, she never took the time to notice. Then one day, on a day like many others, her perfect illusion was shattered.

The day had started normally enough. Hula awoke at 5:00 a.m., showered, dressed, woke her children to make sure they made the bus on time, and then left for work by 6:30. Her commute took an hour and a half, and she spent that time listening to audiobooks or playing soft music as she walked herself through the details of her upcoming work day. As always, Hula felt a twinge of anxiety as she drove along the highway, but she had long dismissed it as simple work stress or frustration about the regular heavy traffic along her commute.

At the coffee shop down the block from her office, Hula sighed in frustration at the line of people waiting to order. Though the length of the line was not unusual, Hula had been feeling more and more frustrated about the wait over the last several months. When she finally approached the counter, she delivered her order to the cashier in a short, angry tone. When the barista handed over her coffee, she ignored his cheerful farewell. Clearly, he hadn't been in the city long enough to know that New Yorkers didn't care for such pleasantries.

As she rode the elevator to her floor, Hula felt her anxiety growing. These were her last few moments before her team would rush her with a dozen questions and a hundred things gone wrong that needed her solving. And this morning would be even crazier than usual because they had a presentation due to a new up-and-coming client early that afternoon. Hula sipped her coffee and tried to steady herself for the day ahead.

As expected, she had barely walked into the office when a half dozen questions were flung at her from her panicked employees. Hula answered questions as she made her way to her office and set down her briefcase and beverage, took off her coat, and sat down at her desk. By

8:15 she had already put out one fire and was moving onto the next.

After she had answered all the most urgent questions her team had for her, she walked over to consult with her graphic designers in their cubicles, where they were engaged in a heated debate about whether the final font selected for the main text of the ad was appropriate with the new ad layout. The copywriters preferred the previous font for their words, while the graphic designers argued that the new style looked better with the overall composition of the piece. Hula sighed and did her best to smooth the ruffled feathers, reminding them that the decision had already been made and that the eleventh hour was not the appropriate time to make significant changes to client presentations.

No sooner had she solved this dilemma than a flustered employee on the verge of tears informed her that the presentation charts and handouts were still in production in the printing department after a disruption to the wireless network delayed all print jobs. Without missing a beat, Hula swallowed her own panic and told the admin to call the nearest print shop to put in the emergency order; she would swing by and pick up the presentation materials on her lunch break.

Hula spent the rest of the morning handling similar near-catastrophes, then rushed over to the print shop on her already-too-short lunch break to be back in time to set up the conference room. As she lay the last presentation handout in place on the long conference table, she sighed as she realized that her job was only beginning. Facilitating the presentation was her most important role, and she had only a few minutes to work up the energy and enthusiasm necessary to impress the new clients.

When all was said and done, the clients seemed pleased but not overly excited about her team's work. As they filed out of the office, Hula's manager lingered behind to speak with her. With a tone of displeasure, he told Hula that she should have been perkier during the presentation and that she'd be lucky if they landed the account at all with her attitude.

Hula was crushed. After years of delivering her highest performance to her company, she couldn't believe the lack of appreciation her boss had just shown. She felt that no matter what she did, no matter how many long hours and missed family events she gave to the company, it was never good enough. Though her department's numbers were slipping a little lately, they were still among the highest in the organization, and she had never lost a client account under her watch.

Hula tried to shrug off the comment and get back to her work day, secretly chiding herself for being so sensitive. Yet the feeling hung like a rock in her stomach for the rest of the afternoon and followed her into her car on the drive home. As she pulled onto her street and thought of facing her children and husband, to her dismay, hot tears started to stream down her face.

Not wanting her family to see her in this condition, Hula pulled up in the park near her house and sat to sort through her emotions. Why was this hitting her so hard? she wondered. She'd had plenty of gruff, ungrateful comments from her boss like this before, so why would this one possibly matter?

As she tried to release and breathe through her emotions, Hula was surprised to find that she began crying even harder than before. Feelings of degradation and humiliation washed over her and she wondered why she had put up with such treatment for so long. She deserved better than this, she realized, and soon anger surfaced alongside the shame. Her sobs became angry screams. When she had worn herself out with crying, her tears were replaced with a feeling of emptiness. Though she was no longer crying uncontrollably, the emptiness was almost worse as it followed her home and darkened her interactions with her family for the rest of the night.

Hula awoke the next morning with a terrible headache and a high fever. The empty feeling was still there. Without her usual determination to push through her discomfort, Hula called in sick to work and settled in to spend the day in bed. The gray, snowy weather outside suited her gloomy mood as she tried to sort through her feelings from the previous day.

As Hula reflected on the day leading up to her breakdown, she recalled a feeling of anxiety underlying every moment. Her job was so stressful that this anxiety was to be expected, or so she had thought, until she started to reflect on how the feeling carried over into her evenings and weekends. Now that she thought about it, Hula couldn't remember the last time she had felt truly relaxed. Even on her last family vacation, she hadn't been able to let her work stress go entirely.

Hula realized that her anxiety was masking a feeling of being trapped. She felt like a slave to her job. It was as though her time—and her very life—belonged not to her, but to the company. Any time she spent to herself felt like time taken away from her job, and she no longer felt any sense of reward for all her hard work. In fact, the more Hula thought about it, the more she came to realize that she didn't even like her job anymore!

As the snow fell down in thick, heavy flakes outside her bedroom window, Hula sat in the silence of her revelation. How long had she been feeling this way? she wondered. Now that she was being honest with herself, she realized that this had been a long time coming. The anxiety she now felt was once a thrill of excitement, a sense of purpose she got from her career. She wasn't sure what had changed or when, but the more she thought about it, the more apparent it became that the signs of her true feelings had been there all along.

Over the last few years, Hula noticed herself growing more tired, more easily stressed and frustrated, less excited about going to work, and less productive when she was there. Her numbers had always been strong, though lately, they had fallen somewhat. She blamed it on the economy, or on her team, but never did she think that it was a reflection of what was going on inside of her.

As Hula began to see all the signs of her unhappiness with greater clarity, she realized that she had always felt that something was wrong.

Yet she ignored the feeling and covered it with more work, more errands, more distractions to keep herself busy so that she would never have to face her true emotions. Now that she felt the terror of the unknown as she realized she needed to do something about her situation, she understood why she had avoided this confrontation with herself for so long. Could she stay at this job now that she knew how unhappy it was really making her? What about all the time she had put in there? What about her benefits and her retirement fund? How would she help support her family if she left? Would things be different with another firm, or would she end up feeling the same as she did now?

The unanswered questions sparked a rising panic in Hula as she began to wonder if she was really happy with her life at all. Had she wasted all these years? Did she ever want anything else that she kept hidden from herself in an effort to please her parents and win their approval? She thought of all the stories and articles she had read lately about people leading alternative lifestyles, traveling full time or running their own businesses. She realized that her family and community had led her to value a life of security and normality, but that she had never stopped to ask herself if it was what she wanted, too.

What she did know was that she could have realized all this much sooner and with less shock and pain if she had been more honest with herself and taken the time to examine the feelings that were underlying her anxiety and overall dissatisfaction. She resolved to listen to herself more carefully in the future. She wasn't sure what to make of all this, but she at least knew that she was closer to her personal truth than she had ever been before.

Chapter 3
Discovering What We Do Want

O nce the immediate shock of her revelation wore off, Hula was left with the aftermath of what she had discovered. The days and weeks following her breakthrough deepened her sense of dissatisfaction with her career and her current life. A part of her had hoped that what she was feeling was only temporary and that after her bad day she would snap back to her old self. Yet the feelings remained, and she found that instead of feeling better, she only felt worse as the days went on.

A month had passed when Hula finally came to terms with the fact that there was no going back. She had glimpsed an unmistakable truth and it would be foolish to try to pretend that everything was okay. Now that she was aware of her frustration and boredom, the feelings hit her more sharply than they had before and she was no longer able to distract herself from them as she had in the past. When she really thought about it, however, she wasn't so sure that she wanted to distract herself from them. She felt that she knew herself better than she had in a long time, and she was reluctant to let go of her truth, as painful and uncomfortable as it might be.

On top of her frustration and boredom, Hula also sensed a vast feeling of emptiness inside of her. It was some time before she realized that she was mourning the loss of the sense of purpose and fulfillment that she'd had before. The feeling had disappeared soon after the novelty of her new career had worn off, and she was saddened to realize that she was grieving something she had lost many years ago. It was as though she was mourning the ghost of a loved one who had passed away years before without her knowing.

After what seemed an eternity, she finally found herself thinking less about the past and all the time she had lost without knowing her true feelings. Hula started to wonder how to move forward into a new future. If this job, this life, this career, weren't what she wanted, what *did* she want? Did she even know how to dream anymore?

Am I having a midlife crisis? Hula found herself wondering. *Am I no different than all those other people who buy overpriced cars and cheat on their spouses to compensate for their sense of hopelessness and desperation?* The more that Hula thought about it, the more she realized that she wasn't like those people at all. The sad truth was that most people never have the kinds of revelations that she did. If it hadn't been for all the self-improvement books and articles she'd read, she might never have had her realization, either. She felt pity for those who went through life dodging the confrontations with their true selves and died as strangers to their very souls.

Well, it was all good to have her awakening, but what was she supposed to do now that she'd had it? The question lingered in her mind, haunting her night and day as she struggled to find the answer. *"What do I want?"* she asked herself over and over again.

So far Hula was only able to identify more of what she *didn't* want. She didn't want to go on feeling trapped in her circumstances. She didn't want to feel that she was putting so much of her life into a career that was ultimately unfulfilling. She didn't want to keep feeling so undervalued and unappreciated for the hard work she was doing. Maybe she didn't even want to have to answer to anyone anymore. She certainly had the skills to branch out as a freelancer, but was the path of the entrepreneur really the one she wanted to walk?

One day when she was browsing social media, Hula scrolled past a meme that caught her eye. She scrolled back and clicked on the image, which was a picture of a magnificent mountain lake with the caption, "What would you do if money were no obstacle?"

The question perplexed Hula, but she felt something stir deep within her. The question both frightened and exhilarated her, for she had barely ever dared to ask it to herself. Sure, she and her husband spent plenty of afternoons and evenings dreaming about the future when they retired. They talked about the properties they might buy, the cities and countries they might visit, the hobbies and pastimes they would take up. But what if she didn't have to wait until she was old to do what she truly wanted? What if she could do it now?

Just as her heart started to warm to the question, Hula pushed it away in fear and frustration. These were fantasies, meant for wealthy kids or those super humans who gained celebrity status, not for her. She had a family to support, after all, and she needed to keep her head out of the clouds and only consider practical options that would help put food on the table.

Yet as hard as she tried to stay "serious," Hula found herself daydreaming in her idle moments at work about being somewhere else—in a cottage in the woods, in a mountain cabin, in a seaside home, exploring a foreign city, or even ziplining through the rainforest canopy. Every time she caught herself in these daydreams, she scolded herself for acting like a college idealist.

Almost as frequent were her fantasies about working from home on her computer, meeting with clients in the mornings and afternoons and being home on time to greet her children when they returned from school. She imagined spending her mornings cooking big family breakfasts and packing their lunches instead of leaving to begin her long commute while they were still rubbing the sleep from their eyes.

Every once in a while, Hula would catch herself daring to dream of turning to art full time, perhaps selling some of her paintings and taking up professional photography. These were certainly the silliest of her dreams, she thought, remembering her mother's warning so many years ago. She didn't even know if she had that creative spark in her anymore, so long had it been since she had lost herself in the creative flow. Yet there was something overwhelmingly alluring about giving herself up to pure creation, to create something beautiful for its own sake and not because she was assigned to.

On the better days at the firm, Hula found herself feeling slightly guilty for considering leaving. After all, she had put so much work into building herself professionally. Despite her boss's rudeness, even he couldn't deny that her reputation was impeccable. Her network was extensive and she had forged genuine connections with her coworkers. The thought of leaving them almost felt like a betrayal, though she was sure they could find her replacement amongst the eager and talented young professionals she had groomed within her team.

And she couldn't pretend that the firm hadn't rewarded her handsomely for her successes. She had risen through the ranks based on her merit, her benefits package was extremely competitive, and her bonus grew each year with every successful marketing campaign her team participated in. Maybe she didn't have to leave to feel happier. Maybe she just needed to change how she did things, or how she saw things. She wasn't sure.

Hula continued to soul search, hoping that the answer to the question of what she really wanted would come. She knew that the most important thing was having the courage to ask the question in the first place. Though she tried not to focus on the negative, she eventually came to see that identifying what she didn't want through the process of elimination was a crucial step in her exploration. She resolved to keep looking, reading any book or article that offered advice as she continued to search for her answer.

Chapter 4
How Big Do We Dare to Dream?

As the weeks dragged on, Hula felt that she was no closer to figuring out what she wanted to do with her life. The options that sounded most appealing were too impractical, while those that sounded more realistic just didn't spark her interest. Though she had tried different approaches to improving her current situation, she found herself coming up short every time. No matter what changes she made, she continued to feel undervalued, overworked, and unfulfilled.

Just as she was beginning to wonder if she would have to resolve herself to always feeling dissatisfied, an unexpected epiphany came as she listened to a podcast one morning during her drive to work. The speaker, an energetic young entrepreneur, was giving a talk about reaching for one's dreams and turning them into reality. "You are only capable of accomplishing what you allow yourself to imagine," he said. "As long as you give in to the fear of whether your dreams are realistic, you will never allow yourself to fully explore the opportunities available to you."

The speaker went on to explain that people too often deny themselves the chance to dream as big as they can. "Society has us so conditioned to toe the line and stay inside the box of the tried and tested that we never allow ourselves to branch out and realize our full potential. Fear," he said, "has stopped countless innovations before they were even conceived.

"Yet the world's greatest heroes have always been the ones who didn't listen to that fear. That's not to say that they weren't aware of the risks. No doubt their peers reminded them of those risks every step of the way. But rather than allow those risks to limit their own possibilities, they chose instead to push beyond the known limits of what was believed to be possible. And *that's* how theirs became household names.

"The moral of the story," he concluded, "is that great things never come from playing it safe. And you'll never have a great idea if you don't allow yourself to dream big. So, go out there and get crazy. Don't just unscrew the lid, blow it right off. Get wild. Dream huge. Think of things that others will call impossible. Then make it your mission to prove them wrong."

As the podcast ended, Hula felt the weight of the young man's words hit her full force. With a flash of guilt, she realized that she had been preventing herself from dreaming as big as she could. It was true that she didn't have the freedom to take the same risks that young, single entrepreneurs did, but was she using her responsibility to her children as an excuse to avoid dreaming big? A well of mixed feelings bubbled up as Hula asked herself this question, ranging from shame to annoyance to outrage. As unpleasant as the mixed bag of emotions was, she allowed them to wash over her, having vowed to explore her feelings as thoroughly as possible.

Hula thought about how her inability to think outside the box was preventing her from envisioning a different future for herself in her current career. Whether she chose to stay with her current firm or left to find another one, she had always imagined her circumstances remaining the same. She began to see that to conceive of a real change in her work situation, she would need to dig deeper and learn how to change herself. To be happy working for someone else, she would need to change her relationship to her work, and to change her relationship to her work, she would need to change her relationship to herself. She wasn't sure how to go about bringing this change, but knowing this much was a revelation unto itself.

Hula also realized that her guilt about her responsibility to the firm and to her family was holding her back from dreaming wild dreams about a vastly different life for herself. She didn't know much about freelancing, starting her own business, or exploring other alternatives, but she knew that she would never learn what opportunities were available to her if she didn't get out of her own way and fully allow herself to explore every option.

She had heard stories about people who retired in their 30s and people who made money from YouTube and Instagram. Then there were those who saved money and sold all their possessions to travel the world full time. And what about those who started their own businesses, built them from scratch, and went on to become the CEOs of multi-billion dollar companies?

Hula wasn't sure that she had any million-dollar ideas, but as she had just learned, she would never know if she didn't even let herself try. As she allowed herself to explore the possibilities in her mind, she felt the whole world open up before her. For the first time, she dared to believe that anything was possible, and that she might just be able to accomplish anything— and that meant *anything*—that she set her mind to.

The feeling was both exhilarating and terrifying, and she had no idea where this line of exploration would lead her. One thing was for certain: now that she was dreaming big, Hula felt a spark of passion reawaken inside her.

Chapter 5
Changing Our Mindset

Over the next couple of weeks, Hula allowed herself to continue brainstorming every possibility for herself. Her ideas ranged from joining another firm to setting out as a freelancer to starting her own company to going back to school to becoming a professional full-time artist to becoming a marketing instructor to switching careers entirely.

She was interested in learning ways to make passive income and retire early, or possibly even finding out how to spend extended periods of time traveling with her family, but she didn't know enough about those avenues to do much more than dream. She had tons of research to do, but every time she grew excited enough about an idea to want to learn more about how to make it happen, she found herself hesitating.

Part of her hesitation stemmed from the fact that she had yet to approach her husband with her thoughts and concerns. Though she had talked to him about feeling discontent in her job, she hadn't yet worked up the courage to admit the true scope of her thinking to him. Derek had worked himself up into the position of senior executive for a major food distribution corporation, and his job came with about as much stress as hers did. With his company still struggling to recover from the recession, the last thing he needed to hear was that she was thinking about quitting her job and doing…well, she wasn't sure what. But deep down she knew that she couldn't make plans for her family without involving them.

As her dreams began to take more shape and her urge to act on them grew more pressing, Hula knew that the time to start communicating with Derek about her ideas was drawing near. Derek loved her more than anything next to their children, and she knew that he would ultimately be supportive of whatever she decided to do as long as she planned it out carefully. Yet every time the opportunity arose to initiate the conversation, Hula found other things to talk about.

One night as she hesitated during a natural lull in their conversation, wondering whether she should bring up her ideas, Derek sensed that something was on her mind.

"Is everything okay, babe?" he asked, a note of concern in his voice.

"Oh, yes," Hula replied hastily. "I'm sorry, hon, I've just got a lot going on at work right now. My mind is still at the office."

Derek sympathized and the conversation naturally turned to work and the latest news from their separate companies. Inside, Hula chided herself for being such a coward. Why couldn't she just spit the words out?

Hula decided to draw herself a hot bath before bed that night. As she soaked in the scented bubbles, she agonized over the question. She knew that Derek would be supportive, so why was she so afraid to broach the topic of making a change? She watched the bubbles begin to pop and fade into a milky mist across the surface of the water. Soon all the bubbles had vanished, and she was left with only a white film to give evidence that they had ever existed at all. Just as the water was beginning to grow cool, she understood.

As long as she never shared her ideas with anyone else, she would never risk being disappointed. Derek couldn't burst her bubble, so to speak, if she never showed it to him. Her dreams were sweet as long as the possibilities remained endless, but talking about them was the first step to making them real—and by making her ideas real, she was risking failure.

With this revelation, Hula realized that it wasn't Derek's doubt or ridicule she was afraid of—it was her own. She was afraid of speaking her ideas aloud and thinking that they sounded stupid. She was afraid of psyching herself up to a course of action that would ultimately fail. She knew that Derek would follow her lead when she came to him with a solid plan. He had known her long enough to trust her judgment, and she certainly felt he believed her to be competent and responsible. He wasn't the one she needed to convince to have faith in her—she needed to convince herself.

The rest of that week was so hectic at work that Hula hardly had time to contemplate the matter further. Even on her long drives, her mind was spinning with upcoming tasks and projects. It wasn't until that weekend that her thoughts returned to the subject. Hula curled up on the couch one afternoon as the kids were playing outside to do some quiet reading on her tablet. As luck would have it, the homepage on her browser recommended an article about a new book that had come out, *Mindset: The New Psychology of Success* by Dr. Carol Dweck.

Always on the lookout for new self-improvement material these days, Hula clicked open the article and began to read the book review. It didn't take long for her to realize that this book might hold the key to helping her confront her fear of failure, for Dr. Dweck's work dealt directly with how successful people related to failure.

Hula had barely finished the article before she downloaded the book to her tablet and began reading hungrily. The insights revealed by Dr. Dweck's research were groundbreaking, and Hula was eager to learn how to apply them to her own life.

As Dr. Dweck's research found, people generally fall into two categories in how they relate to success and failure: some people have what she calls a "fixed" mindset, while others display a "growth" mindset. People with a fixed mindset believe that all their talents, skills, abilities, and personality traits are fixed or determined early on. From their perspective, people don't change very much over the course of time. Some people are born more intelligent, more outgoing, better at math or sports or writing than others, and while people can generally improve on the things that they're already good at, no amount of practice can change their abilities significantly.

People with a growth mindset, on the other hand, believe that with enough hard work and effort, they can change anything about themselves. With practice, they can become smarter, pick up new skills and talents that don't come naturally, change aspects of their personalities, and so on.

The major differences between the two types of people come into play in how they relate to success and failure. Because people with a fixed mindset have hard beliefs about themselves and their abilities, they seek evidence that supports their beliefs, and turn away from situations or evidence that contrast their beliefs. For instance, if someone believes that he is very intelligent, he will avoid situations where he might feel ignorant or incapable. A bad grade could throw him into a crisis if he thinks that it might mean he is not as smart as he has believed.

Those with a growth mindset, on the other hand, take failures to mean that they need to work harder to improve their abilities. Someone with a growth mindset will take a bad grade as a sign that she needs to study harder, work more closely with her instructor, and find exercises to improve her skills. She doesn't see success as being dependent on her natural talents but believes that she can accomplish anything she sets her mind to with enough dedication.

Whereas people with a fixed mindset feel that success is a matter of natural ability, those with a growth mindset see it as a matter of effort. Fixed mindset people see failures and setbacks as a threat to their beliefs about themselves, while growth mindset people see them as opportunities to learn from their mistakes, to grow as people, and to improve their performance in the long run.

The book went on in much greater detail about the differences between the two mindsets, and as Hula soaked in all the information, she felt her fears of failure easing. She knew that she was one of the people who fell into the "fixed mindset" category. She'd always had good grades in school and chose subjects that she was naturally good at. She realized that though she worked hard to get things done, she never put in as much effort as others. She saw now how she had avoided those subjects that challenged her, only doing the bare minimum required for her major and sticking to the subjects she knew she would excel in.

Even in her current career, she had been stressed by the amount of work to be done and felt the pressure of working under deadlines, but she had never truly felt challenged by the work that was expected of her. That lack of challenge could be part of why she was feeling bored and unfulfilled by her career—perhaps a part of her wanted to challenge herself to grow.

It was becoming clear to Hula that what she was really seeking was some sort of large-scale change. Perhaps she would decide to stick with her firm or at least stay in the marketing industry, but she would need to try taking on a drastically new role that would challenge her and force her to grow. Then again, she might also take on the challenge of starting her own business or exploring a new field altogether.

Armed with this new knowledge about the different mindsets, Hula made a promise to herself that she would do everything she could to change from a fixed mindset to a growth one. Rather than fear failure and allow that fear to hold her back from making big changes, she resolved to embrace any failures as mere growing pains. In fact, she soon found herself somewhat eager to make mistakes so that she could learn from them and find ways to improve. This latest revelation was like a gift and she felt lighter than she had in years. She knew that it wouldn't be long before she was ready to make the big changes she had been craving all along.

Chapter 6
Taking the Leap

As Hula's excitement and confidence grew, she couldn't help but be aware of the many obstacles that would face her no matter what she decided to do. Money, of course, was the main concern since whatever change she pursued would need to be lucrative enough to match her current salary. If she decided to go in a direction that wouldn't match her salary, she would need her family to be willing to downsize, which would involve selling their house and moving to a more modest neighborhood. It would be an adjustment for everyone, and she would have to find a way to compensate for asking them to make such big changes on her behalf.

If she decided to go back to school to learn a new set of skills, she would have to somehow find the time to fit classes around her already packed work schedule. Changing positions at her current firm would probably be easy enough, but it could be months or even years before a suitable opening arose.

Searching for a new job entirely would also take some time, since she would need to find a suitable replacement company with a good reputation and competitive salary and benefits package. She had a list of other requirements for her job, such as finding an environment that supported innovative team synergy and working for a company that practiced ethical business and eco standards. This was not to mention the extremely competitive nature of the job market today. While she felt that her resume would make her a top contender for any position she applied for, she might need to update her skills and modernize her habits to ensure her marketability.

The more that Hula thought about the many obstacles she faced, the more overwhelmed she became with the prospect of change. Though she had tackled her paralyzing fear of failure, she was starting to experience paralysis of a different kind—what some experts called "paralysis by overanalysis."

The problem was that she had so many options available to her that it was difficult to choose a single course of action. Each had its own perks and causes for excitement, but each, as she was painfully aware, also came with its unique set of challenges. Hula started to wonder if perhaps the timing for a change wasn't quite right. Maybe she should wait a little longer and keep her eyes open for any opportunities that might arise. Letting fate decide the next step forward wasn't a bad plan, she thought, and decided to settle in for the long haul.

A few months passed and nothing changed. Hula saw coworkers come and go. Some would transfer to another department or division within the firm, while others would leave to join another company. She even lost one of her top team members to another position. Each time someone made a change, she felt a pang of regret. She might have applied for one of the new openings, if only she had known about it. She was too busy to spend time scrolling through job postings online, she told herself. She was hoping that she would hear about an opportunity through others and that the timing would be right for her to apply.

After a while, though, it was starting to become clear that the passive approach was not working out as well as she had hoped. It had been naïve to hope that the perfect opportunity would simply fall into her lap, and she had wasted even more time by doing nothing.

On her way home from work one evening, Hula decided to turn on her favorite podcast. This week's episode was about creating and taking opportunities, and she was eager to hear what the show's host had to say on the matter. As always, he hit his audience with some spot-on advice.

"The question we need to get in the habit of asking ourselves more and more is, 'What would I do if absolutely nothing stood in my way?' Because therein lies the truest, deepest question that has the potential to get us to the heart of our most genuine desires. We tend to spend our time thinking about all the obstacles and barriers that will prevent us from getting what we want—so much so, in fact, that we stop seeing our dreams and only see the barriers that stand in the way of them.

"But here's the truth of the matter: as long as you choose to focus on the barriers and let them stop you from taking action on your dreams, all you will ever experience is a series of brick walls. Because those barriers won't get out of your way until you start to push them.

"If you've been telling yourself that you're waiting for the perfect opportunity to make the change, that things just need to be a little more favorable before you're willing to take the leap, then I have some hard news for you. Your life will never provide you with the perfect opportunity to make a big change. Life is messy. It always has been, and it always will be.

"You will *always* be too busy, but if you really want the change, you need to make time anyway.

You will *never* see the perfect opening that will allow you to make that big change in such a way that it won't disrupt your current flow. Any change you make is bound to blow your life to pieces—and you need to accept that, as uncomfortable as it is, this will always be a good thing. Because it is in that state of chaos that you have the greatest ability to create something completely new.

"So, stop waiting around for the perfect opportunity to make the change. The perfect opportunity will be the one that you make for yourself. That's when you'll have the greatest level of control, when you make a change that you are ready for.

"You don't have to take my advice. The choice is yours to stay where you are or do something big. It doesn't have to start out big. Small steps are often the best ones to take at first. But if you want to see a change, you do have to make that first step, and you can't afford to wait too long to take it."

Hula paused the audio to absorb what she had just heard. The host could have been talking directly to her! And he was completely right; all the obstacles she was allowing to prevent her from taking her first steps were simply excuses that she was using to avoid having to make a change.

As much as she regretted all the time she had lost over her hesitation, she realized that the last several months had given her plenty of time to brainstorm options and really make sure that this change was something she wanted, rather than a passing phase.

She didn't want to think of the elapsed time as a waste, either. In a relatively short time, she had grown profoundly in ways she had never before imagined. She felt that she knew herself better than she ever had. Although she still wasn't sure exactly what she wanted to do, she knew that it was time to take her search to the physical level and start making it real. It was time to brush up her resume, to hit the job boards, to research different graduate programs, to acquire some new skills, to learn about freelancing and starting small businesses. She would even take the time to research the mechanics behind realizing some of her more fantastic dreams, such as traveling full time or generating enough passive income to retire sooner rather than later.

Hula wished that she had had these revelations much earlier in her life, but she couldn't regret the experiences that had led her up to this point. Deep down she knew that everything before now had its own value, and she was excited to see what new chapter she would create for herself. She resolved to speak with her husband that very night about what was on her mind, and to announce her intentions to make a big life change, whatever it would end up being. She would take the leap and create her own opportunities, rather than waiting for life to open the right doors for her. And she couldn't wait to get started.

Part II

What Your Boss Never Wants You to Know

Chapter 7
We Work to Serve Others

As Hula expected, her conversation with Derek went very well. She knew that she was lucky to have such a loving and supportive husband who was eager to see her start this exciting new chapter in her life. Derek had remembered the day that she came home crying from work and was glad that the experience had inspired her to do something different. He asked if she would tell him about everything that she learned as she explored her options more thoroughly and started making plans to bring her ideas to fruition. Hula agreed, happy that she could share her journey with her partner rather than keep all her thoughts to herself.

Whatever she decided, Hula knew that she would need to find work that would keep her busy and engaged. Idleness was not an option for her. Hula had always thrived on hard work, and even if she explored options for early retirement, she knew that that simply meant she would find something else to do with the time she would create for herself.

Since changing directions entirely would take a fair bit of time and careful planning to execute, Hula decided to try to find ways to improve her current situation first. After all, she still wasn't 100 percent decided on leaving the firm, and even if she did, traditional employment through an established organization was always a strong option.

Hula found that the best starting point for her would be to fine-tune the skills that she already had and to pick up a few more that would give her a sharper edge over any competition she would come up against. If she treated this effort as a second job, it shouldn't take much time for her to improve. She would spend any free time that she had beyond her new second job on researching her other areas of interest.

Although Hula had been in management for some years, she had grown into the position through time and experience, rather than going down a management track as a career focus. The firm had, of course, run her through their own management trainings, but the training she had received was specific to the company and she might need a more well-rounded management education to change industries if that was what she decided. She thought it would be a good idea to read some books on management theory to begin.

As Hula read through the various bestselling management texts on the market, she found that she was familiar with most of the concepts presented, either through her company's training or through what she had picked up intuitively from experience and observation. However, she eventually picked up a book that challenged everything she thought she knew. The book was called *The E-Myth Manager: Why Management Doesn't Work and What to Do About It* by Michael E. Gerber.

Early into the book, Gerber upset everything she thought she knew not only about management, but the institution of work in general. Unless you are the CEO of a company, he asserted, you are working to serve someone else. Gerber went on to elaborate that the CEO of a company is the one who has the vision that is the organization's guiding light, while everyone else who is employed there simply works to support his or her vision. This management model has been around since the dawn of civilization, and it has not changed much in all that time.

In order to make this model work, employees must accept the CEO's vision as their own. Yet the truth is that the boss's vision will never truly be their own, and that sooner or later, this truth will make itself known to each individual. Each person will experience this truth in his or her own unique way, whether through a feeling of boredom, restlessness, frustration, emptiness, or lack of fulfillment, but the effect will be the same: the person will never be fully happy working for someone else.

Hula let this assertion sink into her worldview; it certainly was a lot to take in. She didn't like the idea of having spent her whole career working to serve someone else's vision rather than her own. She thought back to her feelings of being unappreciated and undervalued and remembered feeling that any time spent away from work was not truly her own, but was instead time that she was taking away from the company. The more she thought of this, the more the feeling of entrapment and servitude described by Gerber started to resonate with her.

Once more, Hula felt all the negative feelings that were compelling her to make a big change in her career. Although she didn't like the feelings that were coming up, she felt that Gerber had hit the nail on the head, and she continued to read on.

Chapter 8
No One Is Happy Until
They Learn to Serve Themselves

Fortunately, Gerber went on to recommend a solution to the problem brought up by working for someone else. The key to overcoming the lack of fulfillment that comes with serving someone else's vision is to shift inwardly from serving the vision of another to serving one's own vision.

We will never be happy until we find a way to work for ourselves, Gerber asserted. Without our own unique mission and vision, we will spend our lives feeling enslaved to the will of another. So long as the CEO is pouring all of his or her obsession into realizing his or her vision, all of the employees will naturally follow suit—at least, if they hope to keep their jobs. The irony of this was that the appetite of the CEO's vision would never be satiated. It would always require more and more, and the jobs required of the employees would only make it more impossible to fulfill completely.

The employees will become so consumed by the CEO's vision that they mistake that vision for their own. This is a necessary response to a job's requirements of time and commitment—otherwise, how could otherwise autonomous beings be expected to labor away so hard for someone else of their own free will?

Eventually, however, the mind will wake up to this state of being, and the individual will rebel against his "captivity." Of course, people must still find a way to support themselves and their families, so quitting their jobs entirely isn't always an option. Neither can every person in the world expect to start her own company to follow her unique vision.

What people *can* do, however, is find a way to be their own bosses regardless of their work situations. Rather than spending their lives serving someone else's vision, people must find a way to serve themselves. No one can be truly happy until she finds a way to put herself first and to serve her own desires before all others.

Hula reflected on this next bit of advice. She had to admit that she was skeptical about whether it was possible to serve oneself first while still serving the needs of an organization. Nonetheless, she was intrigued by the notion. Although working for another person was definitely seeming less appealing than before, she couldn't help but wonder what advice Gerber had to offer on the subject of putting oneself first in tandem with the demands of working for a fast-paced modern company.

Chapter 9
Understand the Roles that Fear and Desire Play in Life

Gerber's next assertion was a bold one: everyone, regardless of who they are, is motivated by fear and desire. The fear of lack and insecurity is what propels people to assume roles that are unnatural to them, such as submission and a willingness to serve the vision of another. Desire, or greed, on the other hand, is what pushes people to be ambitious and go above the bare minimum required to just get by.

Even CEOs are motivated by fear and desire. Though they seem to have everything by the time they've built a successful organization, they are constantly being pulled by the fear of losing everything they've built. The volatility of the market, the fragility of the global economy, and the constant threat of competition will keep them pushing ever forward. Their desire to achieve greatness and to take their vision as far as it will go will play hand in hand with their fears to press full steam ahead. Everyone else aboard must keep up the pace or get left behind.

The employees also feel this push and pull of fear and desire. Reluctance to lose their jobs prompts people to keep showing up and playing by the organization's rules. Desire fuels the ambition that prompts people to compete against one another for the top-paying positions in the company.

These powerful forces at play within everyone are completely natural. Humans evolved to find ways to survive in any environment, and fear and desire were both fundamental evolutionary forces to ensure that survival. Therefore, these drives are universal to human nature and should not be shunned, but should be understood and harnessed for the greatest success.

Hula paused for a few minutes to think about how fear and desire played out in her life. She could easily admit that she had always felt a desire to do well at whatever she applied herself to, whether it was academics, work, or personal activities and hobbies. Although she didn't like to apply the word "greed" to herself as Gerber did, she could even see some seeds of greed within her as she asserted herself to rise up in her current organization. Her ego had put her at the forefront of her team and gotten her noticed by her superiors, which is what positioned her for the various promotions she enjoyed. While many others were certainly deserving of the various rewards offered by the company, she asserted that she was the most deserving, and set out to prove it through the quality of her work.

Despite her ambition, however, Hula could also see the workings of fear behind everything that she did. Because she wanted her managers to think well of her, she knew that the fear of being punished, demoted, or fired always kept her pushing harder. Especially on the hardest days, when she was sick or tired and didn't want to make the long commute to work, fear of losing her income and becoming financially insecure kept her going.

Hula knew that she would have to take a long, honest look at herself to understand the full extent to which fear and desire played a role in her life. When she had a clear picture of exactly how averse to risk-taking and how ambitious she truly was, she knew that she would have a better idea of what the most appropriate move for herself would be.

Gerber certainly hadn't sugar-coated his meaning about the forces of fear and desire, and Hula appreciated his honesty. She knew that exploring those forces at play within her wouldn't be a very comfortable experience, yet she couldn't deny the fact that understanding what drove her to excel would be a crucial step in discovering what would make her happy in the long run.

Chapter 10
What Truly Motivates Us?

Beyond fear and desire, Gerber continued, people are motivated by a diverse range of internal mechanisms. While fear and desire are universal human traits, other motivations are as unique to the individual as the genetic composition of their DNA. No two people are motivated by the same things, so it is up to each person to discover what makes him tick.

The secret to serving oneself in another person's organization is to understand what one is truly motivated by. Clues can be found by exploring the reasons that prompted a person to pursue a particular line of work or to want to work for a specific company. What is it about this job, or organization, or industry that motivates the person to seek employment there?

The universal element inherent within each individual, Gerber pointed out, was the need to find a sense of meaning or purpose in the work being done. People want to feel that they contribute something unique to their workplace. They want to know that they are doing something valuable, something that no one else can do the way that they can. Without this sense of purpose or meaning, people can't feel fulfilled in their roles, and without the sense of fulfillment, the motivation to work disappears.

Hula tried to remember what had initially motivated her to join her current organization. She applied for the internship with her firm because she knew that the company was at the cutting edge of the industry. The thought of being at the forefront of innovation excited her deeply. Hula couldn't deny that ambition to excel in her career also played a role in choosing to pursue the most prestigious opportunity available to her. She sought the validation of her intelligence and abilities that landing a competitive position would provide.

Her ambition certainly propelled her to take on roles with increasing responsibility as she moved up through the company. No matter her role, she always sought to deliver more than what was expected. While fear would have kept her doing the bare minimum to get by, her ambition to fulfill her potential pushed her to do more. Hula understood that she wanted to see what she was really capable of, to find her limits and push past them. She wanted to be the best her she could possibly be.

Yet the walls that she now felt herself coming up against were halting that forward progress. She knew now that this was a big factor in her sense of dissatisfaction. She was no longer receiving the external validation that had kept her moving forward before. She knew that the level of work she was delivering was still among the highest quality in the whole company, yet her manager was reluctant to acknowledge her successes. Did she really need his validation, or was she happy to know that she was a success? Was her boss threatened by her abilities and seeking to keep her from getting farther ahead? If so, how would she get around this obstacle?

Hula also thought back to what had motivated her to pursue marketing in the first place. Her interest in art had prompted her to seek out a career that would give her the opportunity to use her creative abilities. Meanwhile, her mother's warning about finding a job that would put food on the table also pushed her to seek out a career that was in high demand and offered competitive pay.

As Hula reflected on her original passion from her younger days, she came to understand that her greatest motivation was the act of pure creation. She loved to breathe new life into a project that didn't exist before. She lived for the feeling of creating something that no one else could create. When she poured her energy into bringing a work of art or a creative project to life, she reveled in the knowledge that her creation could never be brought into existence by anyone else. Her works were unique to her. They were the physical proof that she existed, that she was special, that she was doing something that only she could do.

Hula was beginning to understand that to feel completely fulfilled in life and career, she would need to find something that would satisfy both her high ambition and her need to create things

that were a unique expression of her. Armed
with this new knowledge, she had no doubt that
she would find a path that was best suited to her
needs.

Chapter 11
How to Work for Oneself in Someone Else's Company

At last, Hula came to the part of the book that tied all the information together and explained how one could serve oneself first while working within a larger organization. Gerber explained that once one understood the roles that fear and desire played and came to know what motivated him to excel, that person would then have the power to use their career as a means to get the sense of fulfillment that he needed. This might mean using a current position to serve one's goals and needs, or it might mean changing jobs to find that fulfillment.

Once a person knew what motivated her, she should then come up with a list of goals for herself. Who did this person want to become? To create a personal vision for oneself, one should never see oneself as being the same person in the future. A vision meant a complete change in the deepest levels of one's being as that person strove to become the best version of herself possible.

When a person had a solid idea of the person he wanted to be, then he could start setting big goals for himself. These goals would come with certain milestones and benchmarks that tracked his progress. For instance, he might want to become a charismatic leader, and being promoted to a management position would give him the opportunity to pick up and sharpen leadership skills. Being promoted to upper management would be an indication that he had succeeded in becoming a charismatic leader, and he could then use his new position to continually improve his current skills and start to build new ones.

Gerber emphasized that this growth process should never be complete. Everyone could always change, grow, and do better, and each person should see it as her life's mission to spend every moment trying to turn into the best her that she could ever hope to be. This level of commitment would take passion and dedication, and though it seems like a monumental task, it is this philosophy that one can hope to live a life of the deepest passion.

Hence, every job, role, or position held an opportunity for the individual to serve his own needs and his desire to grow into the person he envisioned for himself. If he found himself in a situation that was not serving his growth, then he would have to make a change, either internally or externally, to see to it that he could continue to fulfill his personal needs. The job should be serving him as much as he was serving the organization, but no matter what, the individual's personal vision should always come first on his list of priorities.

Hula found it refreshing and a bit foreign to hear someone advocate for selfishness when it came to careers. As both a woman and a mother, she was used to putting the needs of others before her own. In fact, she realized that it was her parents' needs to see their daughter do well in life that had motivated her to pursue business rather than art. Now, this author was insisting that she put her own wants and needs before anyone else's, even that of her employer, and to put the company to the test to ensure that it was serving her in return.

The empowerment that came with this concept was overwhelming. Hula knew that she was a valuable and powerful contributor to her organization, but now she felt that she deserved more recognition and respect for her contributions than she was receiving. The feeling of deserving something from her employer was completely new to her. She had always known that she earned every reward she received, but she was starting to perceive herself as being valuable simply as a human being. She deserved to feel fulfilled by her career, and it was her birthright as it was everyone else's to find a sense of meaning and purpose in life.

She knew that she had a lot of work to do to process and integrate everything she had just learned into her own life. She wasn't sure that she could find a way to serve her own needs and continue to grow in her current position, but she would spend the next several days reflecting deeply on the concept and see if any revelations came to her. In the meantime, Hula was extremely grateful for the insights she had gained and knew that no matter what she did, she would always seek to serve her own growth first.

Part III

When Working with Passion
Means Being Our Own Bosses

Chapter 12
Am I an Entrepreneur?

As Hula continued to explore the possibilities of finding the change she needed through being employed by someone else, the time naturally came when she started to wonder whether she might be more fulfilled by working for herself. A part of her always knew that her progress would be limited by the opportunities available to her within any organization that she chose to work for.

On the other hand, if she chose to work for herself, the only limits she would come up against were her own. Yes, there were the external limitations of the market, the demand for her services, and her ability to meet that demand on her own, but with the right knowledge and creativity, those limitations could be surpassed. The temptation to go out on her own was very strong, but Hula knew that before she explored that path more thoroughly, she would need to answer a fundamental question for herself: Am I an entrepreneur?

Hula set out to answer this question by absorbing as many books, articles, blogposts, podcasts, and videos as she could. Through all her research, she found that the most successful entrepreneurs tended to embody the following traits:

Action-Oriented

Entrepreneurs tend to be highly action-oriented people. While there are those who spend months or even years polishing the perfect business plan, true entrepreneurs tend to be those who jump in as soon as they can and learn and make adjustments with experience along the way.

Self-Starters

Because they don't have bosses telling them what to do, entrepreneurs need to be excellent self-starters. To build a business from scratch requires a sharp focus and a willingness to put in as much work as it takes to get the job done.

Risk-Takers

The most successful entrepreneurs have always been those most willing to put it all on the line. Whether it is their startup capital, reputations, or even their homes, entrepreneurs tend to give their all to see their visions come to life.

Relentless Tenacity

With risk-taking inevitably comes failure. All successful entrepreneurs have experienced their fair share of failure in their careers, but none have ever let that failure stop them from pushing forward. The ability to recover quickly from setbacks and keep pressing on is one of the most important hallmarks of a good entrepreneur.

High Focus

To beat all the odds, entrepreneurs need to have a laser-like focus on their end goals. This focus must propel them to put in the long hours that growing a startup requires. Entrepreneurs destined for success have a tendency to become completely obsessed with their work. They eat, breathe, and dream their businesses, and if they're really lucky, that dedication eventually pays off.

Endurance

Growing a business is never a short-term endeavor. The would-be entrepreneurs are always distinguished from the true entrepreneurs when it comes time to stick with it for the long haul. Those who give up too quickly never reap the benefits of those with the greatest endurance for overcoming challenges and recovering from failure, but for those who have passed the test, they are often the ones to reap the greatest rewards.

Quick to Adapt

Entrepreneurship requires an individual to adapt quickly to change and to adjust their business models accordingly. Business is a fast-paced world, and those who are slow to keep up are the ones most likely to fail.

Open to Feedback

The best way to gauge the changes that are necessary to success is to be open to any and all feedback that comes. Entrepreneurs can receive feedback from friends, peers, coaches, and customers to learn how best to improve. Even the success or failure of a campaign provides important information about what is working and what needs to be eliminated or changed to improve one's chances of success.

Creative Problem Solving

Entrepreneurs face no shortage of problems that need to be solved, and the best ones never give up as soon as a challenge presents itself. The ability to apply creative problem-solving in the real world is also a crucial trait in creating business concepts since the most successful businesses are the first to identify a problem or lack in the society that they then become the solution to.

Not Fitting In

One of the most universal traits of entrepreneurs is their inability to fit in with "normal" society. Their non-conforming attitude not only compels them to set out on their own, but it also gives them the unique perspective to see things that others don't. Standing aside from the crowd gives one the ability to see opportunities that others miss, and it is one of the best inspirations for out-of-the-box thinking.

Hula recognized some of these traits within herself, but she had to admit that many of them did not come naturally. However, she knew that she could adapt to fit the requirements with the right amount of effort, so she wasn't put off by those characteristics that she did not yet possess. She decided to keep exploring this path to see if working for herself was the best option for her.

Chapter 13
Finding Ways to Make Money Doing What One Loves

N o matter where she turned for advice, Hula always found people insisting that the greatest success and happiness came from learning how to earn a living by doing what one loves. The internet knew no shortage of tantalizing stories about cooking lovers who opened successful bakeries, crafters running successful businesses selling their wares, couples quitting their jobs to make handcrafted furniture, musicians making it big by recording from their home studios, writers selling best-selling novels that they wrote in their spare time, and so on.

The more that Hula read, the more tempting she found it to explore avenues to make a living with her art. The internet offered a myriad of platforms for artists and creatives to sell their work, from social media apps to custom ecommerce websites. The possibilities dazzled her, and she dove in to find out what it would take to start a business based on her passion.

One piece of advice that Hula found over and over again was that before one decided to start a business based on her passion, she would do well to make sure that it was something she really loved doing. Writers often spoke about eventually hating the craft they had once loved after doing it for a living for so long. Artists expressed the same despair, as did career musicians and other creatives. The advice was a sobering shot of reason for Hula, and she promised herself that she would think carefully before deciding to try to undertake any one of her passions as a full-time career.

Yet she also found that she didn't have to decide to quit her job and throw herself into selling art full time to still earn some side income from her hobbies. Platforms like Etsy and Ebay offered low list prices so that vendors could build inventory as they had time and not worry too much about meeting a high demand until they were ready. Social media apps like Pinterest, Instagram, and Facebook Marketplace were great free options for marketing one's wears and finding prospective customers. She also found ecommerce sites like Shopify and WooCommerce that were ready to provide all the tools necessary to build a beautiful and effective online store.

In the physical world, she had plenty of options for finding avenues to sell her arts and crafts. She knew a number of shops in her area that offered consignment options where she could display her goods for a small fee upon sale to the boutique or store. Street festivals, art festivals, and farmer's markets were also great outlets for selling her wares at low cost. Although she would have to pay a fee for the vending booth, she could market her goods without the overhead of a permanent brick-and-mortar location. Meanwhile, she could hand out business cards to point people to her online store, if she decided to open one. Perhaps she could even take custom orders for people that she interacted with in person.

Hula was overwhelmed by the sheer number of options available to her for getting her art out there and into the hands of enthusiastic customers. She came to understand that it is now easier than it has ever been for artists and creatives to make money doing what they love, and she couldn't contain her excitement over the possibilities. However, the accessibility of selling meant that there was also more competition than ever to get in front of prospective buyers, who were oversaturated with consumer options. She would need a killer marketing plan to put herself at the front of the line—but luckily, marketing happened to be her forte.

She also found that many of the same principles also applied to freelancing. Should she decide to go the route of freelance marketing consulting or graphic design, the internet also offered a plethora of channels for freelancers and clients to find and hire one another. Websites like Guru, Fiverr, Upwork, Outsourcingwhere, and so on, were tailored to helping freelancers market their services for a small portion of their earnings. She knew that she had the skills and the experience to be a top competitor in any freelance marketplace, though there was certainly plenty of competition to go around. Yet as she read, one of the most important elements of earning a successful living as an independent agent was not just about doing what one loved, but also doing what one was good at. She knew that her finely tuned marketing and graphic design skills fit the bill perfectly for this requirement.

Hula was encouraged by her findings and knew that even if she decided to stick with traditional employment, she always had the option of earning extra income on the side with her art or through freelancing. With renewed vigor, she continued to explore the best advice on how to make an independent career work.

Chapter 14
Kill Procrastination

As Hula continued to explore the option of freelancing and earning income as an independent agent, she found that one of the most universal issues faced by the self-employed was overcoming the tendency to procrastinate. Especially for those who were attempting a slow transition away from a traditional employment situation, it could be difficult to find the motivation to spend one's free time working even more.

Yet the most influential experts on giving freelancers advice insisted that those who truly wanted to earn a living through self-employment were also those who not only found but made the time to put in the extra work. Killing procrastination was not about finding the time to put in the hours necessary to find clients and send out proposals, it was about overcoming the emotional resistance to starting the job.

Hula definitely recognized a tendency toward procrastination within herself. After all, it had taken her almost a year to even get herself to the point of doing active research to explore her options for alternative careers. She read as much as she could on the topic, knowing that it would come in handy no matter what she decided to do.

One of the simplest and most effective pieces of advice she found was to overcome resistance by committing to doing the undesired task for only five minutes. As the experts said, anyone could do five minutes of something. It might not feel like much, but five minutes on a task was certainly better than no time at all. Moreover, finding the will to begin a task was usually enough to overcome that resistance and keep going. Once people get into the flow of doing something, they are much more likely to keep going rather than stop, so the five-minute trick is a good way to fool themselves into doing much more work than they originally committed to.

The underlying concept behind the five-minute tip was the effectiveness of breaking bigger tasks into smaller, easier ones. When faced with huge, overwhelming projects and tasks, people were much more likely to buckle and avoid getting started. However, if one were to break those big tasks into small, manageable steps, it becomes much easier to tackle the tiny jobs. When stacked together, a series of small tasks quickly adds up, and people quickly find themselves making serious progress on projects that initially seemed too large to handle.

One expert suggested an interesting thought experiment for those especially prone to procrastination. This exercise involved a bit of self-guilt since it required the procrastinator to imagine herself a few months in the future. First, she was told to imagine herself a year from now, happily operating a freelancing or independent business. She was surrounded by the fruits of her labor, happily keeping busy and getting by comfortably in life. Next, she was instructed to imagine where she would be in a year if she didn't overcome her procrastination. In general, she would be in the exact same place that she was now, just as far as she currently was from her initial goal. While she could have spent the year building her business and becoming successfully self-employed, instead she had nothing to show for that time. Hula found this exercise to be a powerful deterrent against hesitating to make a change.

Hula spent some time thinking of how she could break her research and next steps into smaller, more manageable steps so that the process would be less overwhelming. She wished that she had come across this advice much sooner in her journey, but looking back, she saw that this was something she had started doing naturally. She thought the five-minute trick was a great tip, and she knew that she'd also find herself using it to get herself started on housework and other chores.

Hula's research on overcoming procrastination led her to tons of other helpful advice for those who chose the path of self-employment, and she was eager to continue her studies with the new advice on how to overcome one of the toughest and most universal obstacles faced by freelancers and entrepreneurs.

Chapter 15
Setting a Work Schedule that Works for the Individual

Another big challenge faced by freelancers and entrepreneurs is effective time management. Hula found that many people were faced with the challenge of effectively managing themselves in the face of so much freedom. Those who set out to be self-employed full time often had a difficult time summoning the self-discipline to put in enough time to run their businesses. Many let other tasks and obligations derail their work days so that the work that should take the highest priority was often the last to get done—if it even got done at all.

Time management experts insisted that the most important thing any self-employed person could do for himself was to establish set work hours for his business. If you want your business to become a full-time job, they said, you needed to start treating it like one.

One of the greatest perks of being self-employed is having the freedom to set one's own working hours. However, for those who need to work with clients regularly, this also means striking a balance between working when one wants to and making oneself available to the clients when they are available.

Another important consideration for setting work hours is working them around other obligations. For instance, many work-from-home parents tend to set their work hours around when their children will be home and when they'll be at school or day care. These parents might wake up before the kids to take advantage of the quiet morning hours, then take a break to get the kids off to school. School hours are great work hours for self-employed parents, as well as late nights after the children have gone off to bed.

Whatever work hours one decides on, the important thing is to commit to showing up at those times. Establishing a routine is one of the strongest elements of effective time management, Hula found. Routines not only create stability, which translates itself to one's clients and gives them a sense of security and confidence in the contractor, but it also helps eliminate a fair bit of decision-making. Hula learned that each person has a limited amount of willpower and focus every day, and that each decision one needs to make over the course of the day diminishes this reserve of mental energy.

Even simple decisions like what to wear or what to eat can take away vital energy from one's work day. This is why many of the most successful people, from presidents to CEOs, choose to wear similar outfits or eat the same thing for lunch every day. It's one less decision they need to make, which gives them the leading edge when it comes time to expend their energy on much more important decisions.

Hula knew that if she decided to go the route of self-employment, she would quickly set regular work hours for herself and start to establish effective routines. She knew that the regularity would benefit her mentally and emotionally in addition to benefitting her business. With this advice, she knew that effective time management was a crucial part of successful self-employment.

Chapter 16
Set SMART Goals

As Hula continued to absorb all the helpful information she could from books, blogs, and podcasts, she found that another crucial element to successful self-employment was setting hard goals for one's business. Several different blog posts introduced the concept of setting SMART goals, or goals that were Specific, Measurable, Achievable, Relevant, and Time-bound.

Bloggers cautioned that too many people set vague, unattainable goals for themselves, only to later bemoan their lack of progress and accomplishment when their dreams don't come to fruition. Pushing oneself to set realistic goals that come with deadlines and commitments is fundamental to succeeding in any endeavor.

To set successful goals, the goals should first and foremost be specific. For instance, saying, "I want to be a great artist," is a lot vaguer than saying, "I want to sharpen my skills and build my portfolio as a fine art painter." By being specific with setting goals, people begin to outline for themselves a concrete plan with actionable steps.

Next, the goals should be measurable. Rather than say, "I want to make a living as a freelance web designer," people would find better success with a statement such as, "I will earn forty thousand dollars per year through my freelance web design business." By setting a specific salary requirement to this goal, progress becomes measurable and the freelancer can begin to set smaller weekly, monthly, and daily goals for himself to achieve the greater goal.

While it may seem obvious, many people don't understand the importance of setting achievable goals for oneself. When we are young, we tell ourselves that someday we'll be "the best baseball player in the world," or, "the greatest singer," or something similar. However, words like "best" and "greatest" are not only non-specific and non-measurable, they are also not achievable. Concepts like "best" and "great" and "amazing" are completely subjective, so there is no way to accurately assess whether one has achieved the goal. However, adding specific and measurable components to a goal, such as, "I will retire at the top of my athletic career with the best batting average of any other ball player," or "I will build a Fortune 500 company that beats the competition at every level of the market," will create benchmarks by which one can measure progress and potentially make the case for becoming "the best."

All goals set must also be relevant to the bigger picture. Though we often have side goals and side projects that we would eventually like to accomplish, these often serve to distract us from putting our energy into achieving our greater big picture goals. Success coaches often advocate for becoming singularly focused when trying to achieve a large goal, such as building a business or accomplishing large career goals. By pouring all of one's energy into this singular goal, one increases the likelihood of success dramatically.

Furthermore, there are goals that seem relevant to the big picture that simply are not. For instance, setting a goal to "post more pictures than any other Instagram user" might seem relevant to one's greater goal of building a large social media following to generate more revenue, but if those posts are not targeting the right market or converting into sales, the goal of posting more becomes a waste of time and energy.

Finally, the most effective goals are always time-bound. By setting a deadline, an entrepreneur indicates to herself that she must work on completing her tasks not tomorrow or a few weeks from now, but right now, today. Putting goals to a deadline enables an entrepreneur to start creating timelines for her tasks so that she can implement a concrete plan of action. Without timelines, it becomes all too easy to allow insignificant or irrelevant tasks to take precedence over those that should take top priority.

A timeline is like a blueprint for one's goals, and working on tasks and projects without putting those tasks into the context of the timeline is like building a house without consulting the plans. It is hard to see where one is going without stacking the progress up against the overall plan. By creating goals that are time-bound, however, a person can move forward with purpose, determination, and organization.

The concept of setting SMART goals was a revelation to Hula. She knew that when she was ready to choose her next path forward, she would be setting specific and measurable goals for herself that were both relevant and achievable. She loved the idea of setting goals that were time-bound as well, for she had already spent enough of her life on floating by, and she was ready to make something happen with conviction and passion.

Chapter 17
Always Have a Plan

Hula's research about setting SMART goals naturally led her to find guidance on careful and effective planning for entrepreneurs. As she learned when studying time-bound goals, a comprehensive plan is fundamental to success for anyone—entrepreneurs, artists, or those working in traditional employment situations.

Planning should happen on all levels, time management experts advised. First, there should be the major time-bound goals that set the overarching direction for a person. Then, those goals should be broken into smaller steps. The first tier of steps should span the length of several years, from ten years to five years, to three and two years, to one. The goals at the end of each length of time should then be broken down further, with the one-year goals becoming quarterly goals, then monthly goals, then weekly goals, and finally, daily goals and tasks.

Success gurus often suggest that sitting down and setting a month-long plan at the beginning of each new month can help one stay on task to execute goals quickly and efficiently. Weekly plans should also be set and adjusted at the beginning of each new work week. As tasks are executed and new tasks arise, new priorities will have to be set and the plan will change.

Many successful professionals admit that they write out the next day's plan at the end of each work day, prioritizing the three most important and urgent tasks at the top of the list. By having a plan in place ahead of time, they show up to work ready to jump into action, without wasting any time or energy trying to decide where to begin.

The daily plan often includes a detailed schedule of when to execute certain types of tasks, such as urgent tasks, recurring tasks (such as checking email), and low priority tasks (such as filing). The plan also includes break times, which are crucial to recharging energy and maintaining focus.

Hula was convinced that building a comprehensive plan for herself was one of the best things she could do. She knew that the organization this brought to her would make her a more effective and productive professional, and she was eager to start applying her new knowledge right away.

Part IV

*Work Hacks to Work
Less and Enjoy Life More*

Chapter 18
Creating Passive Income

As Hula deepened her studies and continued to explore possible paths forward, she found that her research about entrepreneurship naturally led her to find ways to earn income that she could integrate into her life without having to take much time out of her workday. She had stumbled into the world of generating passive income.

Without knowing what she was doing, Hula discovered that she had hit on a topic she was extremely interested in. She hungrily devoured books like *The Four Hour Workweek* by Tim Ferris, where she learned that many people find ways to invest their time and money into business schemes that would pay them fluidly and grow their wealth with little input from them. Saving the money to make an initial investment or building the infrastructure behind a passive income business would take a lot of time, work, and patience, but the people who accomplished the feat were living proof to testify that the effort was well worth it.

Amongst the most common forms of passive income is investment. Hula already knew a fair bit about investing on the basis of working for a company mere blocks from Wall Street, where discussion of investing and speculating was common break room talk. She and Derek were steadily building their investment portfolios, but neither felt inclined to doing any high-stakes gambling with their savings. Hula decided to move on and find other ways to generate passive income.

She found tons of information about earning passive income through blogging. Several bloggers who blogged about blogging boasted about their six-figure incomes. The core concept behind blogging as passive income is to create something of value that is always in high demand that essentially sells itself. Information is always in high demand, and good, credible information is invaluable.

Bloggers often find a special niche of information based on specialized experience or knowledge that they have. They build a website, attract readers through search-engine optimized keywords, and sell advertising space on their websites. As their readership grows, they earn money from the ad revenue. Blogs do take maintenance, and they take a long time to build, but as long as someone is a good writer with interesting and in-demand subject matter with a decent eye for promotion, blogging is a great option for generating passive income. Hula knew that with her marketing, design, and professional experience, she could find interesting topics to write about that would attract readers from around the world.

One of highest trending channels of passive income has recently come to include online courses. With the accessibility of information through the internet, people were turning to self-education more and more as an alternative to formal education. However, the vast amount of information can make it hard to know where to start, or even what all there is to know on any given topic. Hula had experienced this for herself in trying to learn how to learn about different career options. She had been relying on expert advice to point her in the right way, and she came to learn that she was not alone in feeling that need. That means that there is a high demand for affordable, structured education by credible experts.

Online courses usually consist of videos with regular assignments. They often offer forums or question and answer sessions with the instructors for specialized attention. Many bloggers use their blogging platforms to market online courses to earn additional income alongside the ad revenue they generate.

Writing books and e-books is another way that people generate passive income, which requires the initial research, writing and editing time, and an accessible promotional platform to get the materials into the hands of interested customers.

Hula was intrigued to learn about how people even use social media to earn passive income by simply finding a niche or interest that appeals to a large group of people and building a following. Those with the greatest followings are known as industry "influencers," and they collect money from businesses in their niche who want to market their goods and services to their social media following. Hula's mind swirled with possibilities as she wondered whether she could find a niche area and build a social media following to earn passive income on Instagram or Pinterest.

The list of passive income opportunities continued to grow, and Hula was hard-pressed to keep up with all she was learning. With her specialized knowledge and experience, she knew that she could easily start a blog, and perhaps she could even write some e-books or design some online courses and begin marketing them. However, Hula was concerned that she might become too busy to tackle everything on her own if she took on too many new ventures at once. Moreover, she wasn't sure that she had all the skills she would need to make a leap into digital entrepreneurship. She decided it was best to prepare for those possibilities ahead of time rather than get caught up in the middle of her various ventures, so she pressed on into yet another area of study.

Chapter 19
Helpful Tools and Services

Hula found herself spending more and more time on her laptop in her free hours. It almost felt like she was addicted to learning as much as she could about this new world of digital entrepreneurship. Derek and the kids had a hard time getting her attention when she was in the zone with her studies, but she was so absorbed that she barely noticed. Part of her was aware that this was the spark of passion she had been seeking all along, and now that she was finding it, she was reluctant to let it go for very long.

Hula was already dreaming big about creating a business or service that would be in high demand. Despite the allure of those entrepreneurs who swore that they earned a full living with less effort than a part-time job required, she didn't see herself as the quit-life-and-meditate-all-day type. She knew that she would continue to build upon whatever she created and venture into other areas if she chose the entrepreneurial path.

However, she would need help getting to that point. While she had excellent marketing and graphic design skills, her writing skills were somewhat weak. The time would come when she would need an experienced writer and editor to help fine-tune her work. She would also eventually need a web designer and social media expert, for though she could market goods and services in print advertising, she knew that the world of digital entrepreneurship was a different animal of its own.

She thought back to all she had learned about freelancing and wondered if it might be a good idea to hire other freelancers to make up for the skills that she lacked. However, as she browsed the different freelancing websites she had discovered before, she found herself wondering if she might be better off trying to pick up the skills for herself. The more she could do on her own, the less she would have to spend of her own resources to pay someone else to do things.

Hula was strongly considering signing up for a refresher course on English composition and possibly finding some online courses about social media management and web design when she stumbled upon an article about the importance of outsourcing. As the writer pointed out, outsourcing is an important way for people to reduce their own workload so that they free themselves up to work on the tasks that they are best suited for. The fast-paced world of digital entrepreneurship is highly demanding, and the entrepreneur could quickly stretch herself thin by trying to do everything on her own. Not only that, but the time it would take to pick up the skills necessary to do the work would be time-consuming, and she might not ever be able to do as well as a trained expert. In essence, she would ultimately waste her time on picking up skills that could more easily be handled by someone who already had them.

The abundance of freelance websites means that services are both affordable and accessible, so there is really no reason not to outsource tasks that should be handled by someone else. In that vein, Hula also found that she could outsource much of her administrative work by hiring virtual assistants. If and when she built herself to a point where she could no longer take the time to check her email, schedule appointments, and the other menial tasks that a thriving business requires, she could find and hire a trained virtual assistant to keep her business running smoothly. This would free her up to tend to the actual innovation side of the business without needing to get bogged down in everyday tasks.

Hula was relieved and grateful to learn about outsourcing and virtual assistants before she made the mistake of wasting a lot of her time trying to do too much on her own. She was so excited about all that she was learning about digital entrepreneurship that she was ready to dive into brainstorming ideas and building new business platforms. However, she would soon find that her entrepreneurial ambitions would have to be put on hold as life pulled her attention back down to Earth.

Chapter 20
Giving the Workspace a Makeover

Although Hula had been growing more and more excited with the possibility of forging a new direction for herself in life, she hadn't realized that she was neglecting her family in her exhilaration. One morning, however, her neglect became clear when her youngest daughter woke up with a high fever. Sasha had contracted pneumonia when her immune system dropped from lack of proper sleep.

Derek assured his wife that their daughter's illness was not entirely her fault, but she couldn't help but be hard on herself for not being more attentive to the warning signs that her daughter's health was in jeopardy. As she tended to Sasha, she realized that thinking about quitting her job to jump head first into entrepreneurship was irresponsible. She had known that from the beginning, but her excitement had led her to lose sight of her duty to put her family and their security before her own needs.

However, Hula had come too far in her learning to give up the possibility entirely. She simply needed to take a slower and more cautious approach to her decision-making. In the meantime, she had her current job, whether or not she would ultimately choose traditional employment for her future. Sasha's illness was emphasizing the need for her to ensure that she was providing her children with the best healthcare available. Derek's job also offered amazing benefits, but because his career track required him to jump over to a new company whenever he was offered a better position, it had made more sense for them to sign onto the benefits package offered by Hula's company.

With that in mind, Hula decided to start finding ways that she could make changes in her work life that would enable her to spend less time at the office and more time at home with her family. She knew that whatever she found she could apply to both a full-time job and a self-employment situation, so as she sat by Sasha's bed to keep an eye on her breathing, she started to do more research on her tablet to pass the time.

One of the first articles that Hula came across was about the importance of having a well-organized and tidy workspace. She raised her eyebrow in skepticism. It seemed too simple. However, as she read on, she was soon convinced by the writer that an office makeover could be one of the best things she could do for herself.

Just as routines helped to conserve energy wasted on unnecessary decision-making, keeping a well-organized workspace meant that time wasn't wasted on looking for necessary tools and documents. Even the files on one's computer and the email inbox would function best when well organized. The sooner one could find exactly what one needed at the moment that it was necessary, the more smoothly and efficiently work would flow.

Hula browsed through the different do-it-yourself organization tips and office organization supplies with mounting interest. Although she would stay home for as long as it took Sasha to return to full health, as soon as she returned to work, she would make it a point to start organizing her office to maximize her efficiency and reduce the time she spent at work looking through messy stacks of paper.

Chapter 21
Surrounding Oneself with Positivity

As Hula continued to read on about reorganizing the workspace to boost organization and maximize productivity, she also found that there were several ways she could make changes that would help improve her focus. Psychologists have provided tons of information about how one's environment affects her mood and her ability to focus. Interior designers have been utilizing this information for decades to help them choose the best design plans to suit their clients' needs. Hula was eager to access this specialized information and find out how she could apply it to benefit her.

She found that warm colors, such as reds, oranges, and yellows, are best for stimulating creativity and boosting one's energy levels. However, these colors can be distracting and can also create tension between people in high-pressure environments. Cool colors, such as blues, greens, and violets are best for creating a calm atmosphere and maximizing focus. The downside of these colors is that they can cause one to become a bit too relaxed, which could take its toll on productivity.

As Hula considered her own needs, she reflected on how she often found herself staring into space in front of her computer when she should be working. She realized that she was wasting a lot of time cumulatively by working slowly and not staying focused. She needed some combination of focus-boosting décor with stimulating décor so that she could stay both energetic and focused at work. A smooth combination of relaxing colors and bright, upbeat colors would work best for her, so she resolved to take some calming paintings to hang on her wall along with some bright, playful knick knacks to set on her desktop.

The psychologists also recommended finding ways to surround oneself with as much positivity as possible. When people are happy, they have a much easier time staying focused and staying productive. In fact, she found several studies that indicated that the happiest places to work were also the most efficient. Such was the philosophy at Google headquarters, where the whole building was designed to maximize the happiness of some of the world's most innovative and productive employees.

Hula was intrigued to find so much incentive to take the time to ensure her happiness in the workspace. She wondered how she could find ways to spread positivity throughout the office to impact her team, and how much their productivity would improve with a little bit of a mood boost.

After a brief search on Amazon for affordable office plants and motivational posters, Hula turned back to her studies and decided to keep going.

Chapter 22
Becoming Location-Independent

Later that evening, Sasha's fever grew so high that Hula had to rush her to the emergency room. Derek stayed home with their other children, but he called frequently to check in and ask for any fresh news the doctors had to offer. Hula sat stoically by Sasha's bedside, resisting the urge to cry in desperation in case Sasha should awaken and see her in distress.

Hula knew that it was extremely rare for children to die of illnesses like pneumonia these days, but the maternal instincts in her couldn't help but be activated into overdrive. She was more worried than she had ever been about one of her children, and she knew she was lucky to have come so far without any major crises to parallel this one.

The sense of crisis compelled her to wonder whether it might indeed be better for her to be more available to her children at home. As the long hours of the night dragged on and Sasha continued to sleep soundly, Hula found herself too distraught to get any rest. She pulled her tablet out of her bag and started researching more options for working from home to keep herself from spending the whole night wringing her hands.

She discovered that while she had been thinking of freelancing as a more traditional job with the major change being that she was her own boss, she came to find that a variety of online tools would make it possible for her to do the entire job from her computer. Video conferencing services like Google Hangouts, GoToMeeting, and Skype offer a way for professionals to meet face-to-face using the webcams on their devices. Many of these services were even free to use.

Though she had used video chat several times at work to hold video conferences between her team and their clients, she had never considered using it to telecommute to work before. In the event that she ever needed to spend a significant period of time away from the office, such as now, with Sasha's illness, she could simply call into the office on her laptop and still be present at team meetings to direct her employees and offer feedback. People are doing this more and more as technology evolves, and she knew that if push came to shove, her company would allow her to use this technology if it became absolutely necessary.

Hula was also intrigued to learn that more and more companies are using telecommuting to employ their entire workforces. Even large companies like Amazon and Buffer are hiring location-independent personnel to staff their customer service teams. Though these companies couldn't come close to matching her current salary, Hula was starting to understand how different people are able to make the permanent travel lifestyle a sustainable option for themselves. These people call themselves "digital nomads," and they are a mixture of freelancers, digital entrepreneurs, and location-independent employees working regular hours through telecommuting.

Hula's reading helped to soothe her nerves. It helped to know that she had so many options. Just as she was starting to relax enough to feel sleepy, the doctor came in and announced that Sasha's fever had dropped and it would soon be time to take her home.

Chapter 23
Always Seek to Improve

After nursing her daughter back to health and getting back into the usual routine of work, Hula was ready to turn back to her studies. She was still very interested in finding ways that she could reduce her time spent at work so that she could spend more time at home with her family. The health crisis had definitely ingrained the importance of spending plenty of quality time with the people she loved most, and she didn't want to spend a single second more away from her children than she absolutely had to.

One of the most impactful pieces of advice Hula came across was perhaps some of the most obvious and pragmatic, yet least practiced pieces of wisdom she had encountered. The advice came from billionaire Warren Buffett, who was known for saying to always "invest in yourself"—in other words, to constantly seek to improve oneself.

Hula had always been interested in self-improvement, but the way this advice was presented to her was a way to gain knowledge and improve her skills to master her area of expertise. Other than the management training she had explored in her first round of self-education, Hula had been content in the past with letting her knowledge grow along with her experience as she continued on with her company. However, she realized that she could have been doing much more to master her skills and acquire new ones to make herself a more valuable employee, or a more versatile entrepreneur, depending on what she chose.

Eventually, Hula encountered a website called the "No Excuse List," which is an enormous resource for listing free online classes from topics as wide ranging as liberal arts, to business, to academics, to computer programming, to music, and much more. Through there, she found Coursera.org, which offers free online video courses from top universities around the world on business, humanities, science, mathematics, and technology. Her eyes widened at the variety of classes on business, marketing, and entrepreneurship available on this website.

She also found helpful resources like Khan Academy, which offers tutorials on various academic subjects, and she was surprised to learn that MIT now posts all of their course content free to the public on their college website.

It seemed that Hula now had access to more free resources than she could possibly cover in a lifetime, and she continued to find more every day. She knew that no matter which life path she chose to follow, she would always find value in building her skillset.

Though Hula engaged in self-improvement naturally, she liked the idea of adopting it as a personal philosophy. The power that came with committing to her ongoing self-improvement was astounding, and she knew that she would be a student for life from this moment on.

Although she still had many questions to answer for herself before she forged a new path forward, Hula felt herself reinvigorated with passion and a new zest for life. Already she felt that she had accomplished so much, though the journey had been almost purely an internal one.

She had already begun to apply much of what she learned to her current situation, and she knew she would continue the search for the next step forward as she learned and grew more each day. She looked forward to the day when she would discover what came after this moment, but she was content to enjoy the present one while it lasted.

Conclusion

Thank you for reading through to the end! I hope you found the advice in this short story valuable. Hula's character represents the struggle inherent within us all as we seek to find a balance between finding the structure and security we all need to sustain our bodies and the passion and self-direction we need to feed our souls.

I hope you were as invested in reading Hula's story as I was in writing and sharing it. Storytelling is one of the most effective ways of sharing advice and inspiration, and I hope you found a little of yourself in some aspect of Hula's story. To find out about which path she decides to take for herself, either that of the entrepreneur or that of continuing a traditional career track, be sure to keep an eye out for my next book.

Finally, if you found this book helpful or inspiring, chances are that others will, too! A positive review on Amazon will help others find and access the information here, and will be much appreciated. Thanks again, and I wish you the best of luck on your own personal journey of self-discovery.

About the Author

L am Thanh Hue is a 37-year-old entrepreneur who loves to travel and read. A student of life, she aspires to visit 100 countries in her life. As of this writing, she has visited nine. Hue also plans to read over 1,000 books, as well as to give away at least 10,000 books as a free gift to others. Her favorite topics to read and write about are business and self-development.

Literature has been a lifelong passion for Hue, and she finished school as one of the top five pupils in the literature major. Hue created the story of Hula to share valuable lessons from her own life to help guide others through similar situations in the hopes that they will find their sense of purpose in life. Look for upcoming titles by Hue for more insights and advice.

www.ingramcontent.com/pod-product-compliance
Lightning Source LLC
Chambersburg PA
CBHW051523170526
45165CB00002B/587

*9 7 8 1 5 4 8 1 9 0 1 2 5 *